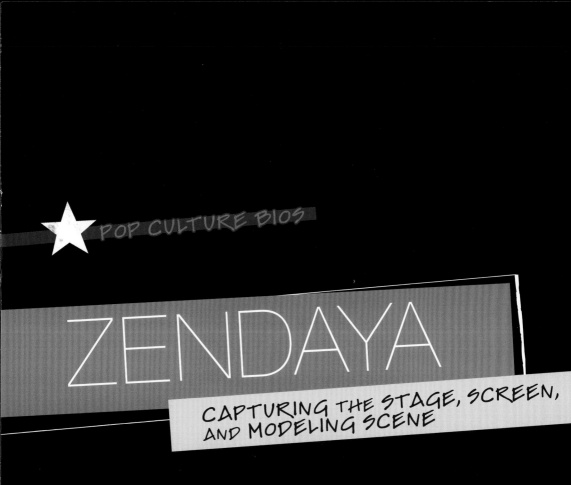

POP CULTURE BIOS

# ZENDAYA

## CAPTURING THE STAGE, SCREEN, AND MODELING SCENE

HEATHER E. SCHWARTZ

Lerner Publications Company

MINNEAPOLIS

Lerner Publications Company
A division of Lerner Publishing Group, Inc.
241 First Avenue North
Minneapolis, MN 55401 USA

For reading levels and more information, look up this title at
www.lernerbooks.com.


Library of Congress Cataloging-in-Publication Data

Schwartz, Heather E.
    Zendaya : capturing the stage, screen, and modeling scene /
 by Heather E. Schwartz.
        pages cm
    Includes index.
    ISBN 978-1-4677-3673-2 (lib. bdg. : alk. paper)
    ISBN 978-1-4677-4735-6 (eBook)
    1. Zendaya, 1996-—Juvenile literature. 2. Actors—United
States—Biography—Juvenile literature. 3. Singers—United
States—Biography—Juvenile literature. 4. Models (Persons)—
United States—Biography—Juvenile literature. I. Title.
PN2287.Z47S35 2015
791.4302'8092—dc23 [B]                      2014004897

Manufactured in the United States of America
1 – PC – 7/15/14

Zendaya (LEFT) and Val Chmerkovskiy (RIGHT) made a splash with their performance on *Dancing with the Stars.*

# INTRODUCTION

Zendaya was nervous. She was in the middle of rehearsing for the TV series *Dancing with the Stars*. She was a featured performer on the show in 2013. Sure, she'd been dancing for years. But her specialty was hip-hop. *DWTS* was something entirely different.

Prepping for the fifth round of competitions, she tried to learn the Argentine tango. She felt far from confident. In fact, she felt more awkward than anything. The moves just didn't come naturally. And the story of the dance had an element of romance to it. Playing that role was tough for Zendaya. She was only sixteen years old. She hadn't experienced true love herself just yet!

Val and Zendaya make a dynamic team!

Working with her dance partner, professional dancer Val Chmerkovskiy, Zendaya struggled to get the moves right. Going into the competition, neither of them believed they were quite ready.

But Zendaya had two things going for her. She was persistent. And she was a perfectionist who could never give anything less than her absolute best. In the end, that combination made all the difference.

Zendaya and Val pose for a pic.

Onstage, performing next to a professional dance couple, Zendaya and Val nailed the tango. The judges didn't miss it. Two of them awarded Zendaya and Val the first perfect scores of the season. The third judge took only one point off. Victory was an amazing feeling. Zendaya was proud, but it was more than that. After the performance, Zendaya told reporters exactly how she felt. Just being onstage was magical for her, she said. And that was the reason she'd loved nailing that tango so much.

Zendaya is a natural-born performer!

Zendaya grew up in Oakland, California.

## CHAPTER ONE

# SHOWBIZ KID

Zendaya pauses for a pic with her parents, Kazembe Ajamu Coleman (LEFT) and Claire Stoermer (RIGHT).

When Zendaya was born on September 1, 1996, her parents named her Zendaya Maree Stoermer Coleman. What a mouthful!

Growing up in Oakland, California, Zendaya spent most of her childhood on or near the stage. Her parents were both teachers, but her mom was also the house manager at the California Shakespeare Theater. Zendaya spent tons of time there, helping out as an usher, selling fund-raising tickets, and studying the craft of acting through the theater's student program.

Zendaya's mom managed the California Shakespeare Theater.

She also soaked in everything she could by watching rehearsals and performances. Sometimes shows were on school nights. She'd plead with her mom to let her stay. Sometimes the outdoor theater was freezing. Still, Zendaya just sipped her hot chocolate and kept her eyes glued to the stage.

## RAISED ON DISNEY

Zendaya's fave shows growing up included *That's So Raven* and *Lizzie McGuire*. She also loved the girl group the Cheetah Girls and even formed her own Cheetah Girls group with some friends as a first grader.

You know Zendaya loves acting, dancing, and singing. But did you know she's also passionate about drawing, writing poetry, and playing basketball? She's a girl of many interests!

## Prepping to Perform

Zendaya attended the Oakland School for the Arts to develop her own acting talents. There, she learned the usual school subjects plus performing skills. She was still a student when she scored some roles in area theaters. At the Berkeley Playhouse, she played Ti Moune in *Once on This Island*. And at TheatreWorks in Palo Alto, she played a male part in *Caroline, or Change*.

For an extra boost of training, Zendaya took classes at the American Conservatory Theater in San Francisco, following in the footsteps of actors Darren Criss, Milo Ventimiglia, and Elizabeth Banks.

Zendaya acted in *Once on This Island* at the Berkeley Playhouse.

Before she was famous, Zendaya was a backup dancer in a Sears commercial starring Selena Gomez. Other backup dancers in the commercial included Ross Lynch and Leo Howard.

## Triple-Threat Talent

Zendaya didn't focus *all* her energy on acting. When she was eight, she danced with Future Shock Oakland, a local hip-hop dance group. She also studied dance at the Academy of Hawaiian Arts in Oakland when she was a kid. On top of everything else, she modeled for stores such as Macy's, Old Navy, and Gymboree.

Once upon a time, you may have seen Zendaya's picture in an Old Navy store!

When Zendaya was about twelve, though, she realized she wanted to focus on an acting career. And she started trying to make that dream come true. Week after week, Zendaya and her dad made the five-and-a-half-hour drive from Oakland to Los Angeles so she could audition for roles.

Her friends didn't always understand her dedication. But Zendaya knew what she wanted, and nothing was going to keep her from going after it.

Zendaya pours her heart into a gig at the California Shakespeare Theater.

## CHAPTER TWO

# DISNEY DARLING

Zendaya and Bella Thorne costarred in Shake It Up.

Zendaya lived life on the go for about a year. Then, in 2009, her hard work paid off in a big way. She auditioned for a new Disney show called *Shake It Up* and landed the lead of Rocky Blue.

Suddenly, her commuting days were behind her. Her days as a student at Oakland School for the Arts were a thing of the past too. She took the role, started homeschooling, and moved to L.A. with her dad. She missed her mom, who had to stay behind for work. Still, Zendaya was getting the chance to live her dream. She felt that was worth some sacrifice.

Zendaya and Bella smile big for the camera.

## STUDENT ON SET

Juggling schoolwork with a career can be challenging for Zendaya. Math is the hardest subject for her. When she's stumped, she turns to her on-set teacher and her mom and dad for help. She feels lucky both parents are teachers!

Zendaya and Bella show off their awesome moves!

## Building New Bonds

As Rocky Blue, Zendaya played a teen dancer who performs with her best friend CeCe Jones. Zendaya sang on the show too, so she got to use all her talents. Actress Bella Thorne played CeCe. Sometimes Zendaya and Bella sang duets. Their song "Watch Me" was released as a single and made the *Billboard* Hot 100 chart.

SINGLE =
a recording of one song that is released to the public on its own and not as part of an album

Playing best friends on the show, Zendaya and Bella got close in real life too. Zendaya told the media she thought of Bella as her little sister. As her career skyrocketed, Zendaya also gained a new "big sister" when she met an actress she'd always admired. **"I was starstruck when I first met Raven-Symoné** because I grew up watching her on the Disney show, *That's So Raven*," Zendaya said in an interview. "She's been like a big sister and mentor to me."

Raven-Symoné is one of Zendaya's role models.

## CREATIVE COMBO

As she got famous, Zendaya dropped her middle and last names. Her first name comes partly from a word that means "to give thanks" in the Shona language of Zimbabwe. Her dad added the Z to make it start with the word Zen.

Zendaya acts out a scene in the Disney Channel movie *Frenemies*.

## Major Moment

Zendaya had made it big with *Shake It Up*. But she didn't sit back and relax once she got to the top. The show naturally led to other opportunities. Her modeling background came in handy when she posed on the red carpet at big events, such as the Teen Choice Awards, and for magazines, such as *Girls' Life* and *Seventeen*.

And she kept working on even more Disney projects. In 2011, she did a guest spot on the show *Good Luck Charlie* and voiced the role of Fern in the movie *Pixie Hollow Games*. In 2012, she costarred with Bella Thorne in the movie *Frenemies* and guest starred as Sequoia on the series *A.N.T. Farm*.

### PET PROJECT

Zendaya has a giant schnauzer named Midnight who weighs about 120 pounds (54 kilograms). She even Skypes with him—and her mom—while on the road.

In August 2012, Zendaya's career took a sharper turn toward music. She signed a deal with Disney's Hollywood Records, joining recording artists such as Selena Gomez, Demi Lovato, and Bridgit Mendler. She was super excited. She'd have the chance to work on an album all her own. She tweeted: **"Epic moment in my life . . . it's official!!! Hollywood Records!!!"** Zendaya's career just kept on climbing.

Zendaya began her official singing career with Disney's Hollywood Records.

Val Chmerkovskiy and Zendaya dance the quickstep on *Dancing with the Stars*.

## CHAPTER THREE

# ALL-AROUND SUPERSTAR

Zendaya and Val dance on *Good Morning America*.

Zendaya belts out a song at a concert.

By early 2013, Zendaya had been dancing nearly all her life. But when she was cast on the show *Dancing with the Stars*, she had to learn a whole new style to compete. Week after week, Zendaya rehearsed with Val Chmerkovskiy. Week after week, they stayed in the competition. Zendaya was psyched to make it to the finals. And even though they didn't win the mirror ball trophy, she left the show happy. She was the youngest dancer ever on the show, and they walked away with second place.

## ZENDAYA'S FAVES

Zendaya has a few favorite things she likes to veg out with.

**TREAT:** coffee ice cream

**SINGER:** Michael Jackson

**TV SHOW:** *Law & Order: Special Victims Unit*

Zendaya uses ChapStick to keep her lips sleek and shiny. She uses liquid liner to create her cat-eye look. She learned how to do it—and perfected her technique—by watching YouTube videos.

## Change Is Good

In July 2013, Disney announced that *Shake It Up* would be canceled after its third season. Saying good-bye to the show she'd been on for so long was a big life change. But it gave Zendaya a chance to shake up her own career too.

Zendaya and Bella Thorne's final *Shake It Up* episode aired on November 10, 2013.

When the show was canceled, she was already set to star in a new Disney movie called *Zapped*, based on the book *Boys Are Dogs*. And in August 2013, she released her own book, *Between U and Me: How to Rock Your Tween Years with Style and Confidence*. It is chock-full of advice for the young fans who look up to her.

Zendaya signs copies of her book, *Between U and Me*.

## Music and More

In September 2013, Zendaya released her debut album, *Zendaya*. She was seventeen years old. Through her music, she tried to show the world that she was growing up.

Zendaya's first single off the album, "Replay," was already a hit. During the summer, it had debuted at No. 42 on the *Billboard*

### ALL TOGETHER NOW

Zendaya's album was a team effort. She helped write the song "Only When You're Close." Other big names in the music business got involved too. The song "Love You Forever" was coproduced by Nick Jonas of the band Jonas Brothers.

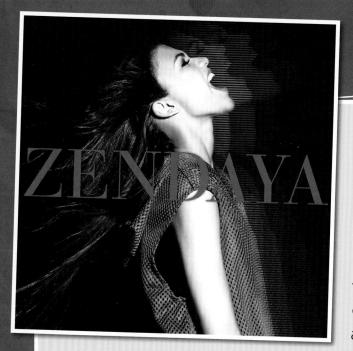

Pop Digital Songs chart. When Zendaya's full album came out, it was well received too. Showcasing a combination of pop and R & B musical styles, the album was edgy. Some critics compared her sound to Jennifer Lopez and Ciara.

Zendaya's voice is often compared to that of Jennifer Lopez (LEFT) and Ciara (RIGHT).

PILOT =
*a test episode of*
*a new show*

In October 2013, Zendaya guest starred on *America's Next Top Model*. She performed concerts to promote songs from her album. But just because she was growing up

didn't mean Zendaya wanted to leave Disney behind. She was cast in the new Disney show *Super Awesome Katy*. It was about a girl who discovers her parents are spies, and Zendaya would play the lead role. In early 2014, she filmed a pilot for the show. She hoped the series would be picked up to air on Disney.

## Up Next

Zendaya has big dreams for the future. She definitely wants to do more with music. She wants to act in films too. But it isn't all about showbiz for Zendaya. She thinks she'd like to start her own fashion line someday and maybe even pursue a career in child psychology.

With talent to spare, who knows what amazing things Zendaya may accomplish? In any case, she's ready for whatever comes next.

## BOYFRIEND OR JUST FRIENDS?

Zendaya appears as actor and singer Trevor Jackson's love interest in his music video for the song "Like We Grown." Rumors in the media claim Zendaya is romantically linked to him offscreen as well. But the two have insisted they're just friends.

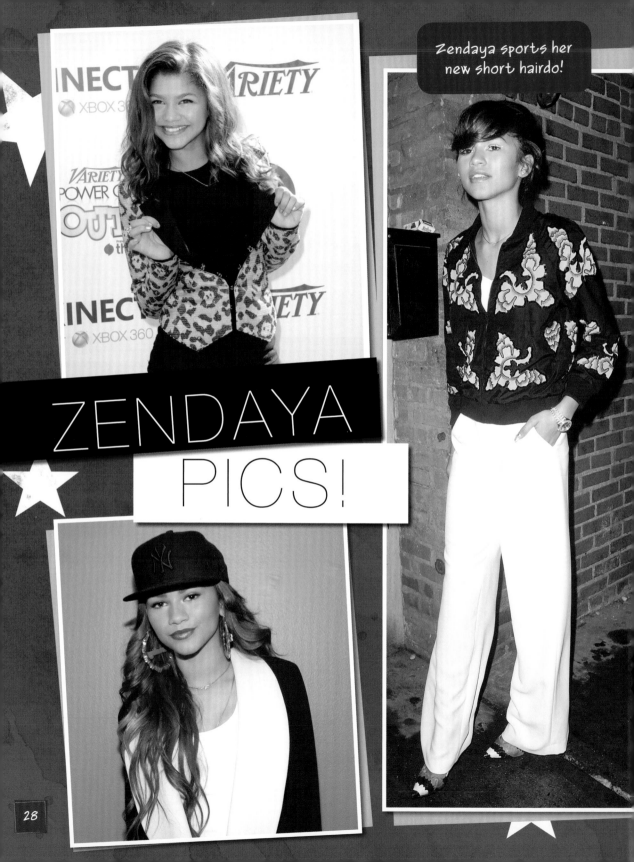

Zendaya sports her new short hairdo!

# ZENDAYA PICS!

Zendaya visits the TV show *Extra*.

# SOURCE NOTES

17 Linda Childers, "Oakland Shakes Up the Disney Channel," *Oakland Magazine*, May/June 2012, accessed February 27, 2014, http://www.oaklandmagazine.com/Oakland -Magazine/May-June-2012/Oakland-Shakes-Up-the-Disney-Channel/.

19 Zendaya, *Twitter*, August 7, 2012, https://twitter.com/Zendaya/status/ 233016311599493120.

# MORE ZENDAYA INFO

Schwartz, Heather E. *Ross Lynch: Actor, Singer, Dancer, Superstar*. Minneapolis: Lerner Publications, 2015.
Read up on Zendaya's one-time fellow backup dancer and fellow Disney star.

Zendaya. *Between U and Me: How to Rock Your Tween Years with Style and Confidence*. New York: Hyperion Books, 2013.
Get advice on life straight from Zendaya!

Zendaya's Facebook Page
https://www.facebook.com/Zendaya
If you're a Facebook user, "Like" Zendaya!

Zendaya's Instagram Page
http://instagram.com/ZendayaMaree#
View Zendaya's latest looks.

Zendaya's Twitter Page
https://twitter.com/Zendaya
Follow Zendaya along with more than 4 million other fans!

# INDEX

The images in this book are used with the permission of: © C Flanigan/FilmMagic/Getty Images, p. 2, 4 (bottom), 20 (bottom left); © Noel Vasquez/Getty Images, p. 3 (top), 15, 29 (top right); © Gilbert Carrasquillo/FilmMagic/Getty Images, p. 3 (bottom), 4, 29 (bottom); © Kevin Mazur/ Getty Images, p. 4; © Craig Sjodin/ABC /Getty Images, p. 5, 16, 21; © Michael Tran/FilmMagic/ Getty Images, p. 6, 7; © Bill McCay/WireImage/Getty Images, p. 8 (bottom); © Richard Cummins/ Getty Images, p. 8 (top); © Jay Yamada, California Shakespeare Theater, p. 9, 13; © Eric Nathan/ Alamy, p. 9; Photo by Ken Levin, Courtesy of Berkeley Playhouse, p. 11; © Patrick T. Fallon/ Bloomberg via Getty Images, p. 12; © Lisa Rose/Getty Images, p. 14 (bottom right); © Jeff Kravitz/FilmMagic/Getty Images, p. 14 (bottom left); © Michael Buckner/Getty Images, p. 14 (bottom); AP Photo/Sipa Press, p. 17 (top); © Matthew Peyton/Getty Images, p. 17 (bottom); © John Medland/Disney Channel/Getty Images, p. 18; © Peter Kramer/NewsWire/Getty Images, p. 19; AP Photo/ABC/Adam Taylor, p. 20 (top); © Debra L Rothenberg/Getty Images, p. 20 (bottom right); © Jonathan Leibson/WireImage/Getty Images, p. 22; © Desiree Navarro/ WireImage/Getty Images, p. 23; © Bennett Raglin/BET/Getty Images, p. 24; AP Photo/Hollywood Records, p. 25 (top); © Jon Kopaloff/FilmMagic/Getty Images, p. 25 (bottom left), 27, 28 (top), 29 (top left); © Steve Granitz/WireImage/Getty Images, p. 25 (bottom right); © Larry Busacca/ WireImage/Getty Images, p. 27 (bottom); AP Photo/Andreas Branch/PatrickMcMullan.com/Sipa Press, p. 28 (top left); © Bennett Raglin/BET/Getty Images, p. 28 (bottom left); © Daniel Zuchnik/ Getty Images, p. 28 (right); © Ray Tamarra/Getty Images, p. 29 (top middle).

Front Cover: © Amanda Edwards/WireImage/Getty Images (large image); © C Flanigan/FilmMagic/ Getty Images (inset).

Back Cover: © DFree/Shutterstock.com.

Main body text set in Shannon Std Book 12/18.
Typeface provided by Monotype Typography.